FOSTER

THE BLIND DIABETIC DOG WHO CHANGED MY LIFE

JACOB KING

CONTENTS

Introduction   ix

1. Meeting Foster   1
2. The Clever Little Guy Settles In   7
3. The Crash   17
4. He's Blind   23
5. Blindness Can't Slow Him Down   28
6. Charisma   32
7. Foster's Legacy   36

Untitled   39

For Foster

INTRODUCTION

All dogs are awesome! Ask any dog lover and they
will tell you the same. But which dog is the absolute
best? That question will get you a multitude of
different answers. When asked that question, some
will speak of a specific breed. Whether it be Yorkie,
Min-Pin, Chihuahua, German Shephard,
Australian Terrier, Xolo, or any one of hundreds of
breeds, ask any pet parent and they will tell you all
about why THEIR breed is the BEST breed.
Others when asked this question will be broader in
their answer. Big dogs, small dogs, medium dogs,
water dogs, herding dogs, terriers, toys... Puppies
are best, adult dogs are best, senior dogs are best...
And then there are those who will tell you that
rescue dogs are the best. I tend to fit into that last

classification. Whether you like them big or small, young or old, pure bread or mutt... It has been my experience that not only are rescue dogs the best, the more of a hard luck back story they have, the more love they will give!

I guess if you were to ask me what the best kind of dog was, I would probably say, "A rescue dog. Specifically, a BLIND rescue dog. More specifically, a Diabetic Blind Rescue dog!" But I'll get to that.

I think it is completely true that the best dog is YOUR dog. You have the best, most loving, smartest, cutest dog on the planet. Funny thing is, I have the best, most loving, smartest, cutest dog on the planet too. In fact, at this exact moment I have SIX of them! But this story isn't about any of them. This story is about one dog. The one dog that started a lifelong obsession for me. This story is about Foster.

1

MEETING FOSTER

I n the summer of 2008, my wife and I went on vacation to New Orleans. It was an amazing trip. It was amazing for many reasons, but one of the things that made it so special was that on this trip we had taken our "Baby

Girl" with us. Our Baby Girl was a three-year-old Yorkie named Coral. The previous year we had taken a trip to Key West, and we had left Coral in a kennel. Mind you, it wasn't just any run of the mill short term pet storage facility. My wife and I had spent the better part of a full weekend visiting every doggy day care and high-end pet resort in our area. We had to be sure that we were leaving our baby in good hands. We had a nice trip and overall Coral seemed to be well cared for, but we spent the entire trip worrying about her and when we got home, we couldn't help but feel that she was upset with us. We swore then that we would never leave her again. So, when the next years vacation came around, we found a very nice pet friendly hotel in the heart of the French Quarter and drove the more than nine hours to get there so that our baby girl could go with us.

At that point in time, Coral was an only child. Well, kind of. We also had a cat named Havana, but she was just a pet. Coral was our baby! When we went to New Orleans we left the cat at home and had a good friend come over to visit with her twice a day. When we got home from vacation, we were feeling a bit guilty for the obvious favoritism we had shown so we went to the local pet mega-mart to buy her something nice. We picked up a few toys and high-end treats for her and before we left we went over to where the adoptable cats were. While I was tapping on the glass attempting to interact with the less than enthused felines, my wife was looking through a binder from one of the local shelters with pictures of available dogs. I heard her yell out, "They've got a yorkie!" I looked at her and she was smiling from ear to ear. I knew exactly what she was thinking. Me being the ever analytical type I said, "If it's really a yorkie I'm sure it's been adopted by now." Her face fell and she agreed that I was probably right. The look of joy falling so rapidly from her face was heartbreaking. I looked around the little table there and found a pen. I then grabbed one of the flyers and handed it to her and said, "Here. Write down the information and we'll call when we get home." She started to smile once again, and I went back to trying to talk to the cats.

After she had the information, we walked on to find a bit more for Havana. All of the sudden it dawned on me. I looked at my wife and said, "Call when we get home? What am I thinking? This isn't 1983, I have a phone in my pocket!" She handed me the information she had written down and I called the shelter.

When the lady at the shelter answered the phone I told her that I had seen Foster's information in the adoption binder and was wondering if he was still available. She said that he was. Shocked, I asked how late they were open. She told me that they were open until 5:00. I looked at my watch, it was 4:35. I said, "We can be there in ten minutes if we can meet him today." She said, "Yes, that will be fine, but I have to tell you before you come. He's blind." For whatever reason, that didn't matter to me. I honestly didn't even think about it, I just told her we were on our way.

We dropped everything we had picked out for Havana where we stood and raced to the shelter.

When we got there we walked in and I said to the lady at the desk, "Hi, I called a few minutes ago. We're here to meet Foster." It quickly became apparent that the lady at the desk was not the person I had spoken to on the phone.

She looked at me a bit puzzled and said, "You're here specifically to see Foster?"

"Yes," I said.

"Did they tell you that he's blind?"

"They did," I assured her.

She then looked even more puzzled and said, "Oh. Okay."

She turned and spoke to a woman who was behind her. "These people want to meet Foster."

The woman at the back said, "Foster? They're here specifically for Foster?"

"Yes."

"Do they know he's blind?"

"They do, they still want to meet him."

"Oh, okay."

She then took a couple steps and opened a door to another room. She said into the room, "There are some people here to see Foster."

From the other room I heard a voice say, "Foster? Do they know he's blind?"

"They do, but they still want to meet him."

A lady came out of the door and looked at us. "Come on back." She said.

When we walked into the room there were cage banks on the left full of dogs. I started looking in the cages when I heard the lady say, "Foster, these folks want to meet you."

I looked away from the cages to where she was. There on the far wall was a desk. In front of the desk on the floor was a dog bed. Above the bed was a sign taped to the desk that said FOSTER. Laying on the bed was an overgrown mop of a dog.

The lady picked Foster up and carried him to

my wife. She handed him to her and as she cradled him in her arms Foster turned his head to the right then to the left. Then he laid his head into the bend of her arm at the elbow and closed his eyes. It was as if he were saying, "Yeah, this will work."

The lady then started to tell us his story. Foster had been found as a stray on a cold rainy winter day in a local neighborhood. He was malnourished, dirty, and full of worms. Thankfully, the person who found him had brought him there since they were a no-kill shelter and if he had been taken to the county shelter in that condition he most likely would have been put down after the mandatory hold. The lady told us that the reason everyone seemed shocked when they heard we were there to see Foster is because not one single person had wanted to come meet him once they heard he was blind. I asked how long he had been there. "Three months." She replied. I got an instant lump in my throat. I looked at my wife and she was crying. I looked at Foster and he was sleeping.

As the tear I had been fighting to contain ran down the side of my face I said, "Let's start the paperwork. I think this little guy has been waiting for us."

THE CLEVER LITTLE GUY SETTLES IN

The very next day I got a call from the shelter. They informed me that our adoption application had been approved! I immediately went to the shelter to pick him up. When they handed him to me he looked at me as if to say, "What took you so long?" I had an instant connection with the little guy. I'm the type of person who loves every dog I see, but this was different. I can't quite explain it, but I knew in an instant that this little guy was special.

I took him home and we introduced him to Coral and Havana. Havana didn't seem too amused and Coral just looked at me as if to say, "He's not staying is he?"

I called our vet and made an appointment to take him in so they could meet him and give him a basic exam to establish him as a patient. I was instructed to not feed him after midnight the night before the appointment so they could do blood work and make sure he was healthy.

When we took him for his appointment our vet took one look at him and said, "I bet he's diabetic." That threw me off a bit. I had never heard of a dog being diabetic. She told us that the cataracts in his eyes were not "old man" cataracts and that when a dog as young as Foster appeared to be had fully developed cataracts like that it usually meant that they were diabetic. She asked us if we had noticed him drinking excessively or urinating excessively. We told her that he had only been with us for a couple days and we hadn't noticed. She asked if we minded if she took his blood to check. I told her as I had many times in the past, "You're the doctor, not me. You do whatever you think needs to be done." She took his blood to run the test and when she came back she said, "Well, his blood sugar is normal. I don't know why he has the cataracts but at least he isn't diabetic."

With an overall clear bill of health, with the exception of being blind, we took him home and we began life as a family with two furry kids… and a cat. As the weeks passed and Foster settled into the family we started to learn about his personality. He was a happy little guy who loved sitting in your lap whenever he could. We also came to find that he loved to play! We had been worried that perhaps him and Havana wouldn't get along, but they did. Havana loved messing with him! One of her favorite games was to sneak up on him and smack him in the head! Foster would immediately go chasing after, barking all the way. Havana would then jump up on the counter and watch as Foster ran all over the house looking for her!

We also came to find that Foster was a resourceful little guy. Determined and smart! He was quite good at figuring things out that I never would have imagined. We took him to visit family so they could meet him and whenever we placed him

9

in an unfamiliar room he would drop his head down and slowly walk around bumping into things and mapping out the room with his head. After a few minutes he would have the lay of the room and he could then walk around without bumping into a single thing.

Then there was the trash. We came home multiple times to find that the trash can in the kitchen had been knocked over and had been rooted through. This had never happened prior to Foster joining the family so we knew it had to be him. It made sense that as he had lived on the streets for who knows how long that he had figured out how to find food. It didn't seem to matter that there was always a bowl of food out for him and Coral to eat as they pleased. So, me being the problem solver that I am, I put a brick in the bottom of the trashcan to weigh it down so that the little guy couldn't knock it over.

That didn't work.

The next time we came home from being out, the trash can was on its side once again. So, I decided I'd have to step it up a notch. I'd make SURE the can couldn't be knocked over. I placed a small chain on the back of the trash can with a clip on the end of it. I then placed an eye bolt on the wall and clipped the can to the wall so that it couldn't be tipped over. I'm smarter than the average little dog… Or so I thought! The next time we went out we came home to the trash can still upright chained to the wall, but there was trash all over the kitchen!

I was determined to get to the bottom of this. So, the next time we left the house I set up an old school camcorder and pointed it at the trash cans. We came home a couple hours later and sure enough there was trash all over the floor. So I went to the video tape. I was amazed and impressed at what I saw. First I saw our supposedly "helpless" blind little yorkie jump up onto the couch all by himself. Then he jumped up onto the back of the couch! I started to panic as I watched, afraid he may fall or walk off the back of the couch without realizing it. I had to remind myself that he was sitting across the room from me as I watched the tape and that he was just fine. He laid down on the top of the couch and took a nap for a bit. This would come to be "his spot" and where you could find him napping most of the time. After a bit, he jumped down and walked over to the trash can. He stood up on his hind legs and sniffed it a bit. Then he grabbed the edge of the trash bag that hung over

JACOB KING

the top of the can and pulled. As he pulled on the bag he began pulling it out of the can and the trash inside started overflowing onto the floor! Once a decent amount of trash had spilled over the side he let go and the trash that remained in the bag pulled it back down into the can so that short of seeing the bite marks on the edge of the bag, one would never know that the trash hadn't just magically jumped out of the trash can. Like I said, this little guy was smart!

From then on we started tucking the trash bag in a very particular way that gave Foster nothing to get hold of and the going through the garbage ended.

That was not however the end of Foster's hijinks.

Our neighbor had a couple of dogs who would often come to visit. We kept a container of treats on the counter just for them. One was a who-knows-what mix named Puddin and the other was a pit bull named Baby Girl. They would come to our back door and sit there quietly until we noticed them. We would hand them their treats and they would head back home happy with their score. One evening we came home to find that somehow the treat container had found its way onto the floor and had been opened. I don't know if it popped open when it hit the ground or if it had been manipulated open but either way there it was. The container had been nearly full of jumbo-sized bone shaped dog biscuits. Now it was now only about half full. Laying on the floor near the container was Coral with her belly looking like she had swallowed a small basketball. She looked just as happy as could be even if she were too full to stand up. Not far away was Foster. His belly wasn't nearly as large and round as Coral's, but it was obvious to tell that he had eaten well more than was agreeing with him.

The next day, Coral was basically back to normal, but Foster was extremely lethargic. I just assumed that it was the doggy equivalent of being tired after overeating like after thanksgiving dinner. Looking back, his condition was most likely much more dire than I was aware.

Over the next weeks we started to notice that Foster was indeed drinking what seemed to be an excessive amount of water. We also noticed that he seemed to have trouble holding his bladder. He had been quite good about going outside to potty since day one. However, it seemed as time went on that he was having more and more accidents in the house.

All of the symptoms that the doctor had described as indications of being diabetic seemed to be showing up in Foster. I called the vet and told her what I had been observing and asked if there was a chance that the test had given inaccurate results. She said that was unlikely, but that anything was possible. We made an appointment for the following day and were careful to not feed him the next morning.

We took him in for his appointment and the doctor took a bit of his blood and disappeared into the back room. A couple of minutes later we heard her exclaim, "HA! I knew it!" She came back into the exam room and said, "His blood sugar is 452! I KNEW he was diabetic!" My wife and I were immediately concerned.

"So what does this mean?" we asked.

"It means we can treat it now that we know what the problem is."

She then began to lay out what having a diabetic dog meant for us. There would be no more leaving a bowl of food out for him and Coral to eat as they pleased. Feeding would have to be done at exact times twice a day. Coral was not going to be happy about that. She had been a free eater since she was a puppy.

It also meant insulin shots. My mother was a diabetic as I was growing up, so I was familiar with the concept of insulin shots, but I had never given a shot in my life. "It's easy," the doctor assured us and explained that we would start with a low dose based on his weight and that after a couple weeks we would bring him back and we would adjust the dosage if needed.

She showed us how to administer the shot and sent us on our way.

When we got home, we took the food bowl from the floor. Coral looked confused when we didn't put it back down. That evening we made up two bowls of food with a set amount in them. We put one down in front of Foster. He started eating. We put the other down in front of Coral. She looked at us as if to say, "Yeah, okay. Put it over there where it goes and I'll get to it later."

I attempted to explain to her that those days were over and that once Foster was done eating I would be taking her bowl away. She just looked at me like I was speaking a different language.

Once Foster was done eating, we picked him up and put him on the counter and gave him his first home administered insulin shot. I'm fairly certain that my wife and I were more bothered by it than he was.

We set him back on the floor and I picked up Coral's untouched food bowl. She looked at me with concern and I told her that I couldn't leave it down there because if Foster got into it before she ate it that it would make him sick. Again she didn't seem to understand. She figured it out pretty quickly though. By the time breakfast came around the next morning she had it all figured out. Eat it while I've got the chance!

Two weeks later we took Foster back for his checkup. His blood sugar numbers were much better, but the doctor said they were still a bit high, so she upped his dose by one unit per shot. Otherwise she said he was looking good.

He was acting better too. His obsessive drinking had slowed down and his accidental potties in the house had all but stopped.

THE CRASH

A few days later, on a Saturday evening I was sitting at the computer when I noticed that Foster was acting odd. It was almost like he was drunk. He was staggering around and was having trouble even standing. My stomach tied instantly into knots.

"Hey buddy, what's wrong?"

He didn't even seem to know I was in the room, let alone talking to him.

"Foster." He didn't so much as turn his head my direction.

"FOSTER!" Again, no reaction.

I looked at the clock. It was after 7:00 in the evening. On a Saturday. There was no hope of getting him to the vet short of taking him to the after-hours clinic which at that point in time I really couldn't afford to do. I called to my wife. "Something's wrong with Foster." I said in a quivering voice. She looked at him and said, "it looks like his sugar is low."

"Is it low or is it high?" I asked. "Either one could cause him to have a reaction and if it's too high I don't want to give him sugar."

I called the emergency vet to ask for advice.

I completely understand their not being able to give any real advice over the phone, but in that moment it was a bit infuriating. All I was asking was if the human blood meter I had there at my house would give me a close to accurate reading on my dog or if it was going to be completely inaccurate. The answer I got from the emergency vet was that I could bring him to them and they would check his sugar, but just the blood test was $50.

Now don't get me wrong. I will spend ANY amount of money to take care of my furry children. I will go without so that they can have whatever they need. However, in that moment that fifty bucks would have turned into a few hundred easy when you figure in that they would have ended up treating him for something. Add in the returned check fee from them if the check didn't go through or the overdraft fees from the bank if it did and I was in a very tight spot.

There I was thinking I was watching my son die in front of my eyes and all I could get from them was, "Bring him in if you think you need to."

I jumped on the internet and started searching. I quickly found that a human blood meter would not give a completely accurate reading but in an emergency situation it would at least let you know if your dog's blood sugar was high or low.

Okay, great! I can use the meter I have. But, how do I get a blood sample from a dog? More searching on the internet gave several different potential options. From pricking the tip of the ear which was supposedly a good option for cats but didn't always work on dogs, to the barbaric option of "quicking" a toenail. My wife was a groomer, so we had the ability to quick a nail, but we also knew that was extremely painful for a dog. Then I saw an article suggesting that you take the sample from inside the upper lip! I thought that sounded like a horrible option. There was no way he'd let me pull up his lip and stick the lancing device in his mouth!

I continued to search the internet and found article after article saying to go for the upper lip! I continued to blow them off until I saw one with pictures and a detailed explanation of how it was done. That article also went on to explain that the inside of a dog's lip has very few nerves and the dog generally wouldn't even feel the prick.

I had to do something so grabbed the lancing device and a paper towel. I lifted his upper lip, dried it off with the paper towel and cringed as I placed the lancing device up to his lip and pushed the button. SNAP! He didn't even flinch and to my amazement there was a nice bead of blood forming that was just begging to be applied to the test strip!

I touched the strip to the blood and the tester beeped... The display on the tester read, "LO!" No number, just LO. I immediately heard the voice of my vet in the back of my head. "Now that we know what the problem is, we can treat it."

I had been meaning to buy some Karo syrup to have on hand ever since Foster was diagnosed as diabetic just in case this sort of thing happened. Unfortunately, I never thought about it when I was at the grocery store and I kept failing to put it on a shopping list. We scoured our pantry and grabbed the best thing we could find. Mrs. Butterworths Pancake Syrup! It would have to do. I put some on my finger and put it in front of his face. I had read that if the crash were too bad that I would have to rub the syrup on his gums and hope that it wasn't too late.

He started to lick. I was ecstatic! He was licking the syrup himself! From what I had read online while trying to figure out how to check his sugar in the first place, next he needed protein. I handed the syrup bottle to my wife and I went to see what I could find. I ended up scrambling an egg.

By the time I had the egg cooked and cool enough for him to eat, he was starting to look better just from the syrup. I placed the egg in front of him and he ate it like it was the greatest thing he'd ever tasted! I took a deep sigh of relief as I watched the life come back to my little guy. It felt like the first breath I'd taken since he first staggered by me nearly an hour before. Again I lost the fight with the tear trying to escape from my eye.

I later found that the particular blood meter I was using would give a reading all the way down to 20. A reading of LO indicated a blood sugar level of 19 or less.

4

HE'S BLIND

As time went on, we settled into the comfort zone that comes with experience. We had gotten Foster's insulin dosage figured out. We had learned the signs he gave when his sugar was too high or too low. We became quite the experts at checking his sugar via his lip.

My wife had found comfort in her abilities as a groomer as well and we decided to jump into the world of owning a small business. I took out a loan from my 401(k) and we started working on opening Furry Kids Grooming!

Previously we had asked our vet if cataracts could be surgically removed from dogs as they could on humans. She told us that they could. In fact it was the exact same procedure but since it wasn't covered by any insurance and the only place to have it done was at the university, we could expect to pay $2500 or more per eye! We fantasized about how great it would be to have Foster's cataracts removed and how humorous it would be when we brought him home and Havana bopped him on the head the first time not knowing that he could see!

When I took the loan to open our grooming shop, I took out an extra $5000 so that we could do just that. We would make Foster see again! We were so excited we could hardly wait. I called our vet and asked her what we needed to do. She said she would make the phone calls needed to get us a referral to the university's vet school and they would contact us to make the appointment.

A day or two later we got that call and the initial screening appointment was made. The morning of the appointment we went to the university and signed in. It was explained that the initial screening would be done that day and we would have to pay $500 up front for the test to be sure that Foster was a candidate for removal. I signed the required paperwork and we went to sit in the waiting room.

As we sat there waiting, we saw a woman come out of the exam area carrying a box. The woman was obviously heartbroken, and she was sobbing deeply. It was obvious what was in the box. I fought to hold back tears for the furry baby I had never met and I hugged Foster a little tighter.

Shortly after, our names were called and we went back. The doctor explained the procedures to us and told us that the initial test would take a couple hours. We were told we could go get lunch and they would call us when it was time to come back.

A couple hours later we got the call to come back and they would discuss the test results with us. We returned to the vet school and after a short wait we were called back. The doctor came out with a stack of papers and started going over the test results with us. She explained that while as far as the cataracts and his eye were concerned, yes, the cataracts could be removed.

However.

Why did there have to be a however?

Per there testing they found that Foster had zero retinal function in either eye. My wife and I were a bit dumbstruck. "What does that mean exactly?" I asked. I was fairly sure I knew, but there was no way I could be right.

"It means that Foster is completely blind." The doctor said.

"That's not possible." I said. "He can see shadows I know. He watches us. When I walk across the room he follows me with his head." I was basically pleading with the doctor. I knew my dog. I knew he could see at least a little.

"We ran the test twice." She said, "His retinas don't work at all. If he is following you with his head, or if it looks like he is watching you, he is following your sound or your scent."

We thanked the doctor and the staff for their work. We picked Foster up and headed to the car. We were both crying as we went. When we got to the car I felt very guilty. I commented to my wife that we were probably the only people crying as we carried our perfectly healthy dog from the hospital. We weren't carrying him out in a box. We should be happy.

5

BLINDNESS CAN'T SLOW HIM DOWN

S o Foster was blind. Completely blind. You'd never know it though. Whether it was jumping up to sleep on his favorite spot on the back of the couch or continually trying to figure out how to get past the latest lever of security I had put on the trash can, Foster couldn't be stopped!

We lived in a small neighborhood that was quite dog friendly. It was nothing to see one of the neighbor's furry kids walking from door to door collecting treats. Since Foster was blind, I didn't want him wandering around aimlessly so I put a bit of a fence in the front yard. I use the term "fence" very loosely here. I had intended to put a fence in the front yard, but there was a city ordinance against it. So I had to improvise. I "edged" our front yard with that white wire edging you buy by the roll. It's more decorative than anything. It's only a foot tall and I think it is intended to keep rabbits out of your flower bed. However, it worked just fine for Foster. For all he knew it was twenty feet tall. From time to time someone would be walking down the sidewalk and see Foster sitting in the yard by the fence. They would say something along the lines of "can't he jump over that?" To which I would respond, "He's blind. Don't tell him how short it is or I'll NEVER keep him in!"

There is, however, always an exception.

Foster got along great with every dog he met. From Coral to the pit bull who belonged to our neighbor Brian, to every dog he met at the grooming shop. Foster was cool with everyone. With one exception. Across the road lived a county sheriff's deputy. Paige. Paige had a boxer named Kilo. Foster HATED Kilo! I don't know why, but it was clear that Kilo was NOT welcome in Foster's yard. One day we were all hanging out in the front of our houses. Me, my wife, Brian, and all of our pups. Then along comes Kilo followed not far behind by Paige. All was cool until Kilo decided to step across the fence and into the yard. Foster was on the other side of the yard. I don't know how Foster knew that Kilo had crossed the line, but he knew! Foster took off after Kilo, barking all the way! Kilo's eyes got huge with a look of shock and fear as he tried to back up across the fence! Kilo wasn't fast enough and Foster ran into him! There was no "dog fight" or "attack" in the traditional since. Foster wasn't biting or even trying to, he was just barking and pushing. Kilo finally found his feet and got across the fence, but Foster wasn't stopping. He kept right on pushing until he himself was across the fence and chasing Kilo across the road and back into his own yard! I took off after Foster! Brian fell to the ground he was laughing so hard! As I got to Foster and picked him up I heard Paige yelling, "DAMMIT KILO! You just got your ass handed to you by a BLIND YORKIE!"

But as I said before, with that one exception Foster loved everyone. He also loved to play. One day a puppy was brought to the grooming shop for her first groom. Her name was Skipper. We set Skipper down to see how Foster would interact with a puppy. It was great! For several minutes Foster and that puppy played. It was hilarious! I absolutely loved watching the two of them interact. Thankfully, I had the presence of thought to pull out my phone and take a video. The puppy was bouncing back and forth in front of Foster's face and Foster was trying to catch her. He did a couple times! All the while, Coral was running to my wife for protection! Skipper tried to play with Coral, but Coral was having none of it!

6

CHARISMA

I've loved deeper than words can express every
furry kid who has ever honored us by joining
our family. I appreciate the terminology in
"pet adoption" as it implies that you are making

32

them a part of your family. I tend to go a step further. Whenever it happens that we are looking to expand our family I don't say, "We'd like to adopt him." I say, "We'd like to invite him to join our family."

I hate it when I hear people say that they "bought a dog." You are talking about one of the most precious forms of life to ever walk upon this planet.

It also infuriates me when I hear people say that dogs don't have a soul. I went to four years of a Christian high school and I can't count how many times I heard that. I wish every one of those people could have met Foster because if ever anyone had a pure soul of kindness, it was Foster. But it wasn't just me. Everyone who met him knew it in an instant. I can only describe it as charisma.

Just prior to the opening of our grooming shop there was a local dog festival called Critterfest. In an effort to promote our new business we had a bunch of give away merch made with our logo and set up a booth.

When we arrived to set up we were given a map of the festival with all of the booth locations on it. My wife noticed that not too far from where we were to set up was a space for a rescue called the

Blind Dog Rescue Alliance. We decided that we would have to take Foster to their booth so they could meet him. Once the festival was up and going, I went to where their booth was to be only to find a vacant square of grass. I made some pathetic attempt at a joke about the blind group not finding the place.

Although they hadn't made it to the event, it would come to be that their name being on the map was enough. I had never heard of them and might have never found them if it weren't for that map. But find them we did, and we became quite active with them for years to come. At the next Critterfest there WAS a Blind Dog Rescue Alliance booth. It was right beside our grooming shop's booth, and we were running both of them.

We had Foster and Coral with us at that first Critterfest event and nearly everyone who visited the booth wanted to pet Foster. He was happy to let them.

I expected that to happen. It was a dog festival, of course there would be a ton of dog lovers there. What I didn't expect was the sheer number of people who came back to the booth with someone in tow saying, "Here's that awesome dog I told you about. You have to pet him." I knew Foster was awesome, but how did they know? We were at a festival with literally hundreds, if not thousands of dogs and yet there were multiple people bringing their friends to meet our Foster.

I was beyond shocked when we returned to Critterfest the following year and had more than one person come to the booth and ask if Foster was with us! They asked for him BY NAME! It broke my heart having to tell them that he was no longer with us.

7

FOSTER'S LEGACY

I won't go into detail about Foster's last days with us. It is a heartbreaking story to hear and an even more heartbreaking story to tell. All I will say it that Inflammatory Meningoencephalitis is a cruel disease.

I don't strive to be the type of person to be

remembered for deep philosophical quotes, but if I am remembered for one, I want it to be this. "The cruelest punishment that God ever bestowed upon man was allowing us to fall so deeply and unconditionally in love with these furry little creatures and then forcing us to outlive them by so long."

Foster only graced our home for a mere thirteen months before he went on to the rainbow bridge. If it had been thirteen years it still wouldn't have been enough time. I love him so much I can't put it into words, but his legacy lives on.

Before Foster I didn't know blind dogs existed. Since Foster, my wife and I actively volunteered for the national Blind Dog Rescue Alliance for several years. I was on their board of directors for a term, and I am still happy to help them when I can today. I hope that as time goes on that I will have the time once again to take a more active role with them.

Before Foster I didn't know diabetic dogs existed. Since Foster we have shared our home with six blind dogs. All but one of them were diabetic. I know there will be many more.

To learn more about Blind Dogs and how you can help, please visit www.blinddogrescue.org

To see the video of Foster playing with Skipper, please visit https://youtu.be/Xmn2V3XnGhg

Made in the USA
Middletown, DE
07 January 2022

58032146R00029